USBORNE KEY SKILLS

Wipe-clean Comprehension

Illustrated by Magda Brol

Written by Caroline Young

Designed by Meg Dobbie

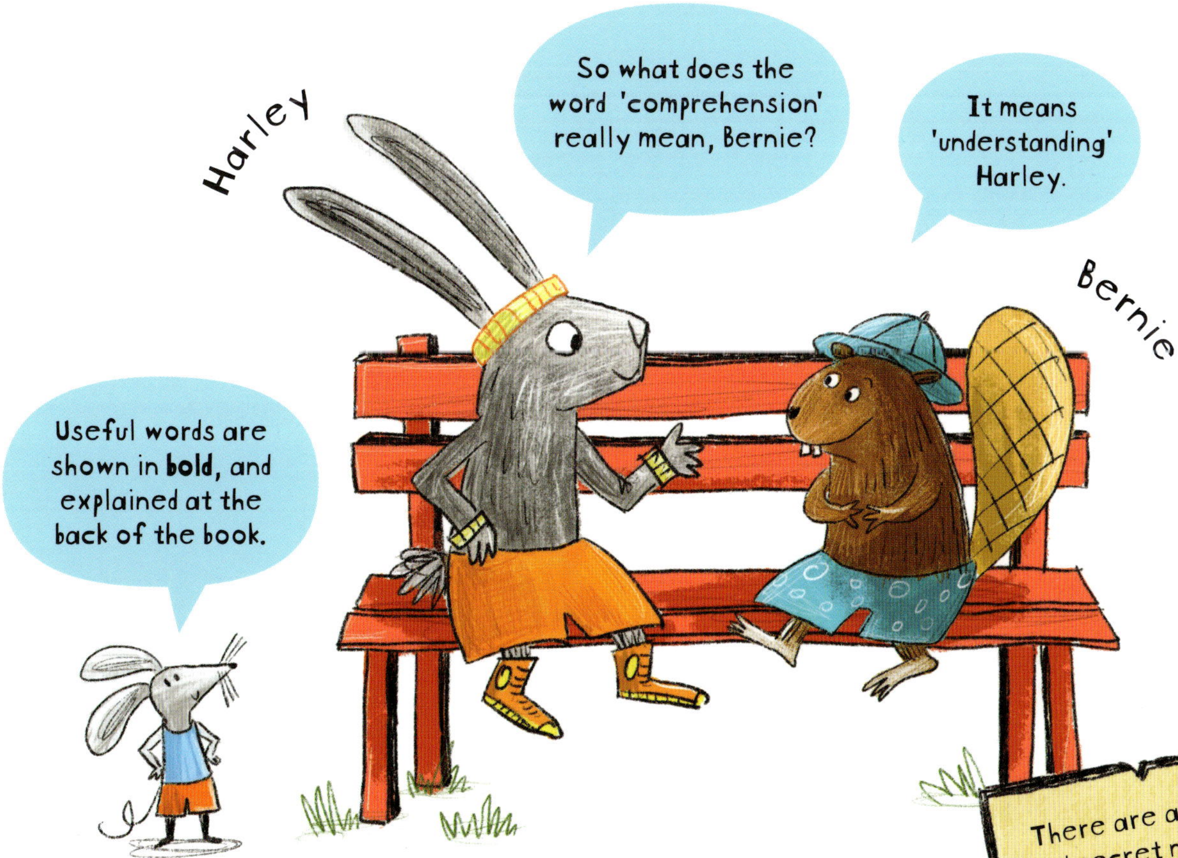

Series Editor: Felicity Brooks

With thanks to Alice Morrison-Lebbon

Good books

Marvin is looking for a good book to read. He prefers **fiction** (which is made up, such as stories and poems), and he especially likes books full of action and drama.

Read the back cover of these books, and circle the one you think he should choose.

Now circle which book you would choose for yourself.

The animals are talking about books they like.

Can you think of a book you really enjoyed? Write its title here.

____

What did you like about it? Jot your thoughts down quickly.

____

____

What would you write on the back cover of the book, to persuade someone else to read it? This kind of writing is called a **blurb.**

____

____

____

____

Exciting explorers

Suki enjoys **nonfiction** books, full of facts. Today, she's reading a book about her great-grandmother, Sophie, who was a famous explorer. When Sophie was in the Sahara Desert, there was a ferocious sandstorm. She wrote this **paragraph** to describe it:

The wind whipped the sand up into a swirling cloud. Each gust sprayed me with tiny grains that stung me, even through my fur. The air was warm, but the sun was blocked out by a thick wall of sand. It was hours before I could see the desert sky again.

Can you imagine it now, too?
Circle the words or **phrases** that helped you.

How would you have felt, if you were there?
Choose three **adjectives** and write them here:

1.

2.

3.

Now, put your adjectives into a sentence or two that help your reader imagine your feelings.

After days in the boiling desert, Suki's great-grandmother reached a shady oasis. Here's a picture of what she saw and some of the phrases she used to describe it:

swaying palm trees	glittering water	patient camels	warm breezes

Can you imagine arriving at an oasis in the desert? Describe it here in a short paragraph, using phrases from this page, or your own if you prefer.

Facts and instructions

Brenda wants to find out about butterflies. She's got a library book, written notes and made some sketches. Can you write the correct sentence next to each picture?

1. This butterfly lays tiny eggs on a leaf.

2. The eggs hatch into little caterpillars.

3. The caterpillars eat and eat and get bigger.

4. Their bodies make a case called a chrysalis.

5. A butterfly forms in the case and starts to break out.

6. The butterfly dries its wings and flies away.

Harley wants to grow carrots, and he's asked Brenda to write him some instructions. She's done some sketches, but run out of time. Can you write a simple sentence under each one so that Harley knows exactly what to do? Here are some words you might need.

prepare soil sprinkle seeds water seedlings crop

____

____

____

____

Why not try planting some seeds yourself? You could write down what you do and how the seeds grow on the fold-out page at the back of this book.

What would you like to grow, if you could? ____________________

Writing letters

Marvin has lost Peck's book, 'Great Woodpeckers through History', and he's worried that she'll be cross. He's written to say sorry, making sure his letter includes the six important things in the box below.

Write the correct number in the six boxes on Marvin's letter. The first one has been done for you.

1. The address he's writing to
2. His address
3. The date when he is writing
4. The name of who he's writing to
5. Main part of letter
6. His signature

[1] Peck's tree
The Forest

[ ] My house
The Forest

[ ] 30th April

[ ] Dear Peck

[ ] I'm so sorry, but I've lost your book about woodpeckers. I've searched the whole forest, but I can't find it anywhere. I promise I'll buy you a new one and that I'll be much more careful with your books from now on.

[ ] Yours sadly,

If you were Peck, what would you reply? Write your letter to Marvin here, with the six important things you need in a letter, all in the right places.

Peck

Is there something you've done recently that you're proud of? It doesn't need to be anything big. Write a sentence about it here.

Is there anything you're not so proud of? Write it down (and wipe it clean straight away, so nobody ever sees it!)

Where shall we go?

The animals want to go on a holiday, but everyone has different ideas.

Peck thinks that she's found a holiday that will suit everyone. Read through this description carefully and then tick 'Yes' or 'No' in the boxes to see if it does.

The reasonably priced campsite is right next to a quiet beach, where you can surf, swim or snorkel. After days full of sunshine and fun, you'll fall asleep at night listening to the seabirds and whispering waves.

	YES	NO
Is it peaceful?	☐	☐
Is it likely to be sunny?	☐	☐
Are there sports activities?	☐	☐
Is it expensive?	☐	☐
Are you near the sea?	☐	☐

What would be your ideal holiday? Put a number 1, 2, and 3 next to the three things in this list that you'd choose, with number 1 the most important.

- ☐ Sunny weather
- ☐ A warm swimming pool
- ☐ Lots of fun activities to do
- ☐ Playing with friends
- ☐ Trying new things

Using the three things you chose, write a postcard about your holiday. (You'll need to make up an address, too.)

Writing a summary

Cody is learning how to write a **summary** (a short version of a longer piece of writing). Here, he's written a summary of a story he enjoyed as a young cub. Do you recognize it?

Once upon a time, a boy called Jack sold a cow for some magic beans. They grew into a huge beanstalk. Jack climbed right to the top, and found a giant's castle. The giant was so nasty that Jack stole all his treasure.

Write the name of the story here, if you know it:

____

Jot down the five main points in Cody's summary in your own words. The first one has been done for you.

1. *Jack got some magic beans.*
2. ______________________________________
3. ______________________________________
4. ______________________________________
5. ______________________________________

Now write the story out in full on the fold-out page at the back of this book, adding as much detail and drama as you can. Add some pictures too, if you like.

Cody's started another story summary, but he can't finish it.
Can you choose the correct word or **phrase** and write it in each gap?

A young girl called Red Riding Hood went to visit her granny in the forest. ______________________________ ______________________________ and saw her in bed, she knew something was very different. She realized that the Wolf had eaten her granny! A woodcutter heard Red Riding Hood's screams, killed the Wolf, and rescued Granny from ______________________________

Everyone (except the Wolf of course) lived ______________________________

When she got to her granny's house	inside its tummy.	happily ever after.

Can you write the five main things that happen in this story?

1 ______________________________

2. ______________________________

3. ______________________________

4. ______________________________

5. ______________________________

What's the story you enjoyed most when you were little? Jot down the five main points in it on the lines above, then write a summary on the fold-out page at the back of this book.

Which word?

Harley and Brenda like learning new words, so they are playing some word games to help them. Why don't you join them and learn some new words too?

You may not know the words in **bold** in this poem. Read it through carefully, and then circle what you think each of them means from the choices in the box.

Some animals in the jungle are **nocturnal**. come out at night/smelly/timid

When the sun sets, they begin the hunt for **prey**. friends/animals to kill/churches

Poised, they wait in the darkness. angry/ready/posing

Waiting for their moment to **pounce**. jump out/bounce/win

Next, Harley sets Brenda a challenge – to write the very best word she can in each gap in this **paragraph.** Can you help her? Here are some words for you to choose from. You can really change the story with your choices, but there's no right answer.

beautiful perfect sang nervous miserable excited
delicious nice disappointing chatted argued
screeched howled gorgeous dark wonderful joyful

It was a ____________ day for a picnic. Everyone was very ____________ and the food was ____________. The animals ____________ all the way. The jungle looked ____________ and the birds ____________.
It was sure to be a ____________ day.

Now choose a word of your own to write in each gap.

In the third word game, Brenda asks Harley to use each of these words in a sentence. Can you help him?

bristly shimmering grim

1. ____________________

2. ____________________

3. ____________________

You can wipe the page clean if you want to write different sentences.

Animal facts

Dilly and Bernie want to find out more about each other, so they start by reading a website all about armadillos. Afterwards, Dilly's going to ask Bernie some questions to see how much he remembers. He might need your help!

First, Dilly asks Bernie to write three ways that armadillos stay safe, in his own words. She tells him to start each sentence with 'They'.

1. *They* ________________________

2. ____________________________

3. ____________________________

Next, Bernie must explain what armadillos eat, and how they find their food.

They ________________________

____

Can you guess how these animals got their names?
Start each answer with 'They'. The first one has been done for you.

1. A blue-tongued skink *They have blue tongues.*
2. A spotted salamander ______________________
3. A white oryx ______________________
4. A rainbow lorikeet ______________________

Now it's Dilly's turn to find out about beavers. Underline two facts in these **paragraphs** from Bernie's book, 'Fabulous Facts about Beavers'.

Beavers

Beavers have transparent eyelids to see underwater. They can breathe under the water for up to 15 minutes.

Beavers' front teeth are orange and never stop growing. They gnaw pieces of wood to stop them from getting too long.

Now write down the two facts you underlined, but in your own words. You might write, 'Beavers can see underwater' for instance.

____

____

____

____

Now choose two different facts and write them instead.

What happens next?

Peck is giving the animals some story-planning tips. She tells them that it can help to think of a story as having these five steps.

How to write a story

1. The start sets the scene and gets the reader interested.
2. Then, something happens to get the story moving.
3. Next, there's a development, or a problem to solve.
4. The story moves forward and the problem is resolved.
5. The story ends and the reader feels satisfied with the ending.

Cody has lots of ideas for stories, but he gets muddled up. Can you help him, by putting 1, 2, 3 or 4 next to these ideas?

- ◯ The animals found a map showing a mysterious secret cave.
- ◯ They had finally found the entrance to the secret cave!
- ◯ They set off, excited but a little nervous too.
- ◯ Slashing through the brambles, they thought they glimpsed a doorway.

Write Cody's four ideas on this planner, in the right order, next to numbers 1 to 4.

Story planner

1. ____

____

2. ____

____

3. ____

____

4. ____

____

5. ____

____

Next to number 5, Cody needs an ending for his story. He has thought of three possibilities. Put a tick next to the ending you think works best and write it on the planner.

- ◯ They are too scared to go into the secret cave after all.
- ◯ They rush home to tell their families all about their adventure.
- ◯ Some friendly animals live in the cave, and invite them inside.

Using the fold-out page at the back of this book, write a story based on Cody's ideas. You can change things or think of a new ending if you like.

You can use the five-step planner for your own ideas any time you want to write a story.

Labels and lists

The animals are holding a sale to raise money for charity. Suki is in charge, but she's too busy to write the prices on the labels. Can you write the correct price on all the things they hope to sell? One has been done for you.

Price list

Books 2 Small toys 1 Large toys 5

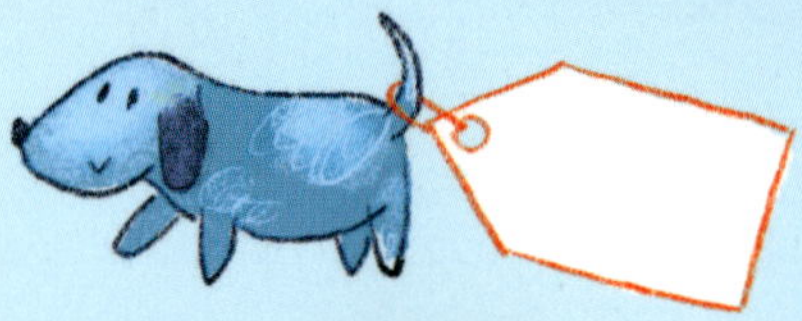

Everything sold! Write a list of what was bought and the price. The first one has been done for you.

Robot	5

Total:

The sale went so well that Harley and Suki decide to hold a cake sale next. Draw lines to match the descriptions to the right cakes.

A delicious, soft chocolate cake

Full of oats, nuts and fruit to give you energy

Crispy, chocolatey and full of crunch

Draw a picture of your ideal cake below, and then write a description of it on the lines.

Now invent a new cake, draw a picture, and write a description of it on the lines.

Comprehension quiz

Now that you've finished all the comprehension activities in this book, try this quiz to see how much you remember. (The answers are at the end, if you need a little help.)

1. The animals are setting up a stall to sell some clothes they don't need. Can you write the correct name in each label?

a) 

b) 

c) 

d) 

e) 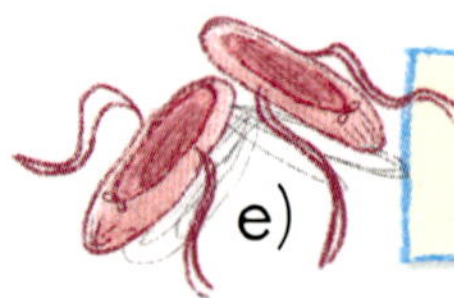

2. Choose the best **adjective** to describe each animal from the ones shown on the green strips below. Circle three adjectives.

a) 

oily tiny spiky

b) 

striped spotty fierce

c) 

cuddly furry scaly

3. Read this paragraph carefully.

If skunks are scared, or trapped, first they lift up their bushy tails. Then they spray anything nearby with a very stinky liquid from their bottoms. The smell can last for up to three weeks.

Now circle the right answer to these questions:

a) What do skunks do first if they are scared? Run away/Turn around/Lift their tails

b) What do they do next? Spray smelly stuff/Growl/Lift their tails

c) How long will you be smelly, if you get sprayed? A day/A week/Up to three weeks

4. **Fiction** books are full of ideas made up by the writer, but **nonfiction** books are full of information and facts. Circle the nonfiction books below.

5. Imagine you didn't know how to wash your hair! Here are the basic instructions you need. Write 1, 2, 3, 4, and 5 in the boxes, to put them in the right order.

- ◯ Turn the shower off and wrap your hair up in a towel.
- ◯ Stay under the shower and rinse all the shampoo out.
- ◯ Get into the shower and get your hair wet.
- ◯ Rub a blob of shampoo into your hair until it bubbles.
- ◯ Dry your hair with a hairdryer if you need to.

6. Read through this **paragraph**, and then answer the questions underneath it.

> There are thousands of words in a dictionary. The chapters or sections are written in alphabetical order from A to Z. There are often examples that show you how a word is used. They help you understand the word's meaning better.

a) What will you find in a dictionary? ______________________________

b) What letter will the words in the 5th section begin with? __________

c) Name one good way of showing what a word means ____________________

____

7. Here's a list of things Harley found in the bottom of his school bag. Can you circle the ones you think he might need, and put a cross through the ones he should get rid of?

mouldy carrot

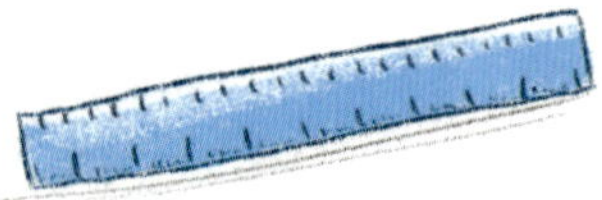
ruler

calculator

pencil case

used bus ticket

reading book

old pen lid

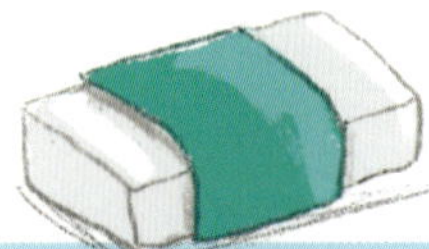
rubber

Quiz answers

1. a) football boots   b) cardigan   c) dungarees   d) hat   e) ballet shoes

2. a) tiny   b) striped   c) scaly

3. a) Lift their tails   b) Spray smelly stuff   c) Up to three weeks

4. Nonfiction titles are: 'Living with Lions: My Safari' and 'How to Grow Vegetables'

5. ④ Turn the shower off and wrap your hair up in a towel.
③ Stay under the shower and rinse all the shampoo out.
① Get into the shower and get your hair wet.
② Rub a blob of shampoo into your hair until it bubbles.
⑤ Dry your hair with a hairdryer if you need to.

6. a) Thousands of words   b) E   c) Giving an example of how a word is used.

7. Things Harley might need: pencil case, ruler, rubber, reading book, calculator
Things he should get rid of: a mouldy carrot, used bus ticket, old pen lid

Score 1 point for each correct answer and write your score in the box.
If you want to get a higher score, wipe the pages clean and try again.

29